The Law of Sevens

A Fitness Program for the Mind

By
Dr. Daniel F. Lavanga

"Finally, someone has *really* been able to point you towards *your own answers*! Dr. Lavanga teaches you how to organize and manage your thoughts and actions to create a greater sense of living. In the <u>Law of Sevens</u> you will be challenged fully. Accept the challenge and a *balanced and inspired life* will be yours!"

Joe Cantando
President/CEO
Integrity At Work, Inc.

"I found <u>The Law of Sevens</u> to be a concise compendium, a quick-read and a highly organized journey through the Universal Laws of Personal and Professional Success. '

Dr. Lawrence T. Markson
The Master's Circle, Inc.

Reading Dr. Dan's book will help you understand that it's not life's events, but our attitude toward them, that turns them into an opportunity or negative experience. Work shopping this book raises your level of consciousness and certainty.

Dr. Joseph Maio
Natural Health Chiropractic

Dr. Lavanga's new book, <u>The Law of Sevens</u>, is an excellent starting point for those beginning the challenge toward self-awareness. And for those already on that path, it can be the next step.

Barry Kassel, Esq.
Elkins Park, Pennsylvania

"<u>The Law of Sevens</u> allows the reader to celebrate the weaver by penetrating the deepest mysteries of the weave. Dr. Lavanga has organized the most profound principles of wisdom so that all who read it can transform, transcend, and evolve. This book proves that all is connected and that there is no limit to what we can be, have, and do."

Lawrence A. Newman, D.C. Esq.
Coral Springs, Florida

To find out more about having Dr. Lavanga speak at your convention or work
with your company, please contact:

Danmar Publishing
112 E. Pennsylvania Blvd.
Feasterville, PA 19053
215-364-1112

Cover Design, Book Layout & Printing: Associated Printing & Graphics

ISBN 0-9749407-0-4

Printed in the United States

Dedication

This book is dedicated to Dr. John Demartini and the teachers and students of the Concourse of Wisdom School of Philosophy and Healing. This school without walls has enabled me to logarithmically expand my capacity for learning, while opening my heart and mind to the magnificence of the world in which we live. More important, I've been given the freedom through The Quantum Collapse Process™ to access the wisdom of the ages as it applies to my healing practice, as a writer and teacher, as a husband, parent, son, and friend. It is also dedicated to all those who ask the questions that will help them be the best they can be.

The good news: There is nothing new in the Universe.

The bad news: The secret of your success is locked up in your heart.

The good news: <u>The Law of Sevens</u> is designed to open your heart.

Introduction

The mission of the author is to open eyes, hearts, and minds to the potential energy available for us to rise above our current paradigms and paradoxes and take on new levels of personal and professional management. We are on the brink of an explosive and magnificent new dimension of the information age: the linking together of the universal principles and laws of quantum physics with human consciousness and the human desire to create a better world for ourselves while making a difference in the lives of others. _The Law of Sevens_ is one of those books that supports our current beliefs and challenges us to move to the next level of consciousness, growth, and freedom. Whether you are in pursuit of spiritual awareness, mental genius, career advancement, financial and business excellence, familial stability, social relationship, or physical well-being, this is the right book at the right time. The goal of this book is to provide you with an effective path to follow in uncovering and pursuing your mission. At the end of each chapter are exercises to assist you in mastering the material presented. The best method for using this book is to first read it through completely, then reread and do the exercises.

The bottom-line results of following *The Law of Sevens* are three-fold:

1. *The Law of Sevens* is an express elevator to finding your mission and integrating it into the seven areas of life and the universal principles of success, gratitude, and unconditional love;

2. The methodologies in *The Law of Sevens* will allow you to place your subconscious mind on an autopilot path to a balanced and fulfilling life. This will ensure that the thoughts you think, the people you meet, and the actions you take will be part of **your** plan for **your** life;

3. The 49 parts of *The Law of Sevens* are a recipe for an extraordinary life. They will help put you in tune and in touch with the highest principles, wisdom, and teachings ever shared on planet Earth from ancient to modern times. If you know where you are going in life, they will help catapult you to the stars. If you haven't yet figured out your mission, *The Law of Sevens* will assist you in getting your rocket to the launching pad.

A Special Thanks

To Marian, Georgie, Courtney, Nicole, Johnny, Donato, Vittoria,

John, and Marie for being my mirror and teaching me how to love

To Mariette and Steven Landry for the editing and the tattoo

To Sandy Francano-Richards for the re-editing

To Don Rubin and the staff

To my patients, clients, and mentors

To Drs Larry Markson, Danny Drubin, Alan Ruosso,

Neil Hollander, Bob Kessler, Stephen Zelinger, Joe Maio,

Al Latronica, Joe Mullen, Mark Pearson, Larry Newman,

Mark Castrantas

To Bill Benz, Jack Boland, Bill Fidler, Helma Lucker,

Mark Lorenstein, Tony Robino, Lillian Zazar, Jason Koscinski,

Jim Donovan, George Schuler, Barry Kassel, Dave Saracco,

Joe Cantando, Ed Shannon, Ed Kent, Bernie Mannix,

Wayne Hileman, Patti Smith, Brian Macnamara, and my

Chiropractic staff past and present

Table of Contents

Chapter 3

Chapter 4

Chapter 5

Chapter 6

Chapter 7

The juggler must maintain peripheral focus to keep all the objects afloat.

Chapter 1

The Seven Areas

1. Spiritual
2. Mental
3. Vocational
4. Financial
5. Familial
6. Social
7. Physical

Life is a balance. The microsystems and macrosystems of the planet on which we live, the body we inhabit, and the universe that encompasses and surrounds us, are in a constant state of expansion and contraction. The purpose of these microcosmic and macrocosmic machinations is to maintain order and balance. There is an enormous amount of energy created and expended in this process. Your priorities in life (value system) determine the results you achieve. It is more effective to have your daily life reflect your values. The fun in life begins when you take on the appropriate level of responsibility, to balance the level of fulfillment you seek. Chapter I and the exercises that follow it will help bring greater focus and power to your day-to-day activities. Balancing your life requires energy. It is a skill, and therefore it takes training and practice. It is worth the effort!

First, let us break life down into its component parts. We will call these the seven areas of life: spiritual, mental, vocational, financial, familial, social, and physical. A thorough mastering of all seven areas is key to a fulfilling life. One of the most effective ways to help yourself is to become aware of the hierarchy of your value system as it relates to the seven areas of life.

To determine the hierarchy of your value system, simply catalogue where and how you spend your time, energy, and money. For example, if you spend a significant amount of time involved in your church with meetings or choir, etc., and the moral or ethical implications of daily life occupy your time, then spiritual development is high among your values. If you spend a significant amount of your time learning, studying, and researching information, or using and improving your mental skills, then the mental area of life is high among your values. If you are working and taking courses to further your career, your identity is linked to your work (you do carpentry work, versus "being a carpenter" is who you are), then vocation is high among your values. If you play the stock market, study the laws governing investments, spend a significant amount of time working on or thinking about finances, then the financial area of life is high among your values. If you spend a significant amount of your time taking your kids to their sporting events, coaching their team, or taking care of your parents, then family is high among your values. If your friends, parties, and social events take a significant amount of your time, then the social aspect is high among your values. If you are concerned about your health and take time to do regular exercise and massage, or take tennis lessons, then the physical aspect is high among your values. That's simple, right? Now, if your highest priority is to advance your career through schooling, but you are spending a significant amount time enjoying the social area of your life and ignoring school, then nothing is wrong, but you will eventually beat yourself up for not focusing enough attention on your career.

A key to self-mastery is understanding that your current circumstances are a result or reflection of your value system. Another key is to have congruence in your value system by linking your daily activities to your mission. Although all seven areas of life are interdependent and interrelated, it benefits us to break them down for purposes of finding where we are incongruent with our values and bringing life back into balance. Another cause of confusion and imbalance in life comes from the inability to effectively switch in and out of the roles we play: mother, father, wife, husband, educator, club member, breadwinner, etc. Developing the skill of balancing roles is most efficiently accomplished by starting with congruency in your hierarchy of values and the seven areas of life.

1. Spiritual

Your spiritual life includes religious and non-religious insights, nonphysical or metaphysical, ethereal or astral plane experiences. The term *spirit* is historically linked to the term *energy*. "En" equals being, "erg" equals a measure of force, therefore energy equals being of force. The spiritual part of our life is the link to the unlimited energy resources available in the universe.

2. Mental

Your mental life includes everything for which you use your mental capacities, such as receiving ideas, projecting thoughts, perceptions, dreams, goals, visualization, focus, and learning. The evolution of the mind occurs when it is open and accomodates to new ideas. Through the evolution of your mental processes, you have a greater capacity to synthesize your physical body's kinetic energy with your spiritual mind's potential energy. The result is an increasing greater ability to tap into the infinite universal resources.

3. Vocational

"What you do in life echoes in eternity" is a line made famous by the film "Gladiator". The career or vocational path you've chosen says a lot about who you are. Also remember that there is no such thing as a "bad" career choice. Every job you have or had has taught you a skill for future use. The extent to which your vocation is congruent with your mission is the extent to which you get to do what you love to do in life. Inside each of us is an unlimited potential, the potential for greatness. We tap into this potential by listening to the voice from within our hearts. Doing what you love to do in life brings steadiness and a quieting of the mind, which allows you to hear this calling and to follow. Connecting your vocation and all the other areas of your life with your mission will add to your level of self-worth and fulfillment.

4. Financial

Your financial life deals with all aspects of your relationships to money and finances. Your financial worth is intimately related to your self-worth. To the extent that you suffer from low self-worth and feel undeserving, you will find a way to sabotage your financial endeavors. To the extent that you have high self-worth and feel deserving, you will attract greater finances to manage. This principle can be applied to all the areas of life.

5. Familial

Your family life includes all the aspects of relationships falling within the dynamics of your bloodline and extended family. The family dynamic will undergo a perfect balance of happy and sad, gain and loss, war and peace, pleasure and pain, rich and poor, and repression and expression. Since family plays an important part in your psychological makeup, it is not wise to undervalue or over-value the role of family in your life.

6. Social

Your social life includes the dynamics of any and all of your relationships outside of your family dynamic. Your social network includes friends, clients, patients, church groups, and business acquaintances, as well as your relationship to your local, city, state, and federal government.

7. Physical

Your physical life includes everything on the physical or mate-rial plane relating to your body. Taste, touch, smell, sight, and sound are the receptors of life that let you know you are physically alive. "I feel, therefore I am." Your physical area of life relates to health, appearance, activity, use or abuse, disease, chemistry, and of course the senses.

Your physical body is the vehicle you have been given to transport you through this life. The human body has the potential to receive and broadcast lightwave vibrations in the physical form through the five senses and in the spiritual or energy form through the mind as ideas and thoughts. You will receive information relating to all areas of your life through your physical body, sometimes in the form of symptoms. When you are inspired and following your mission in life, your body is energized and less susceptible to disease and the aging process. When you are not inspired and not following your mission, your body is de-energized and more susceptible to disease and the aging process.

The juggler develops acute peripheral vision for he knows that if he focuses attention on one object alone, he will lose all the rest. The wise man develops patience, long-term vision, and a global view.

The seven areas, spiritual, mental, vocational, financial, familial, social, and physical are the pieces of the pie, ingredients in the recipe, parts of the puzzle. No matter how you describe them, they were designed to be integrated and to function as a whole. We are here to master all seven areas. When we avoid or over emphasize one, we create confusion, and imbalance, and we attract events, positive or negative, to bring about equilibrium.

Congruency, balance, and synchronicity are the foundation of wisdom and personal power.

The Seven Areas

The most efficient and effective method of accomplishing your goals, achieving your mission, and living a fulfilling life is to have congruency between what you deeply desire and how you actually live your life (value system) in the Seven Areas.

First, determine the level of congruency between your goals/ mission and your hierarchy of values.

Action:

1. To determine your hierarchy of values (desired), list your goals in the seven areas of life.

   Spiritual _____

   _____

   _____

   _____

   _____

   _____

   _____

Mental _____

_____

_____

_____

_____

_____

_____

Vocational _____

_____

_____

_____

_____

_____

_____

Financial _____

_____

_____

_____

_____

_____

_____

Familial _____

_____

_____

_____

_____

_____

_____

Social _____

_____

_____

_____

_____

_____

_____

Physical _____

_____

_____

_____

_____

_____

_____

2   Prioritize the Seven Areas according to the number of goals..

_____

_____

_____

_____

_____

_____

_____

3. To determine your hierarchy of values (actual), catalogue your

activities by percentage or hours per day spent in the Seven Areas.

(Where do you spend your time, energy, and money?)

Spiritual _____

_____

_____

_____

_____

Mental _____

_____

_____

_____

_____

Vocational _____

_____

_____

_____

_____

Financial _____

_____

_____

_____

_____

Familial _____

_____

_____

_____

_____

Social _____

_____

_____

_____

_____

Physical _____

_____

_____

_____

_____

4. Prioritize the Seven Areas according to the estimates of most
    time spent in each.

    _____

    _____

    _____

    _____

    _____

    _____

    _____

5. In order to determine congruency between your goals/mission and
    your hierarchy of values, compare your priority lists in #2 and
    #4. The key to congruency is to match your actual hierarchy of
    values (where you spend your time, energy, and money) with your
    desired hierarchy of values (goals).

6. **Action:** Develop an action plan to shift your priorities (time spent) so that your values match your mission. For example, if attracting a loving relationship is one of your top three goals, but your social life is low on your actual hierarchy of values list, plan more activities in the social area of your life.

_____

_____

_____

_____

_____

_____

_____

_____

_____

_____

_____

_____

_____

_____

_____

Your innermost dominant thought determines your level of consciousness and your destiny.

Chapter 2

The Seven Levels

1. Love To
2. Choose To
3. Desire To
4. Want To
5. Need To
6. Ought To
7. Have To

The Seven Levels are an adaptation of Mazlow's, and Demartini's, hierarchy of needs. They are a reflection of the levels of human consciousness. This is important because our level of consciousness determines our emotional reactions, perceptions, and our destiny. Human emotional perceptions will judge people and events in life consistent with the level of consciousness. These perceptions will move from an unbalanced to a balanced perspective consistent with the level of conscious evolution attained by the individual. Our consciousness will evolve from judgment to indifference to love consistent with our ability to bring our emotional charges (perceptions) into balance. Each of the seven levels correlates with an emotional reaction from desperation to inspiration. Emotional reactions may be preprogrammed or self-taught neurological habit patterns. In this chapter and the worksheet that follows are the tools to discover where you are now and the opportunity to reprogram your consciousness, perceptions, and destiny.

In a 7:1 ratio, we will see seven times more good than bad, or seven times more bad than good, in a person or event. We will be attracted or repelled to a degree consistent with this ratio. In a 6:1 ratio, we will see six times more good than bad, or six times more bad than good, in a person or event. We will be attracted or repelled to a degree consistent with this ratio. This pattern continues from a 5:1 ratio through a 2:1 ratio. As we move from 7 times more attracted or repelled to equilibrium (1:1) the state of mind will transform from chaos, imbalance, and desperation to order, balance, and inspiration. In a 1:1 ratio, the good or bad, positive or negative perceptions regarding a person or event are synthesized into a neutral state. We become grateful for what is as it is, and our heart is opened in love and appreciation. Our emotions are steadied, our mind is clear, and our creative power and growth are maximized.

The Want To 4:1 ratio to the Have To 7:1 ratio are characterized by outer-directed goals, living someone else's dreams, and a perception of the need to bow to social pressures. The Desire To 3:1 ratio to the Love To 1:1 ratio are characterized by inner-directed goals, living one's own dreams, and fearlessness in the face of outer social pressures. The farther down the hierarchy from a 1:1 ratio to 1:7 or 7:1 ratio, the more unsteadiness, brain noise (confusion), ingratitude, disease, and aging we will experience. The farther up the hierarchy from a 7:1 ratio to a 1:1 ratio, the more steadiness, clarity, gratitude, health, and vitality we will experience.

1. Love To Level - 1:1 Ratio

The spirit of unconditional love, *Nirvana*, the space between two thoughts, the following of the inner whisper, following the heart, are descriptions used to define a state of being in which people are doing what they love and loving what they do. Unconditional love embraces the pleasure and the pain of life. The master doesn't let his pain and pleasures keep him from his purpose. The love level is a rare state of inspired living. The more we synthesize the dualities of life, the positive and the negative, the pleasure and the pain, the more love we generate and attract. This leads the mind to a state of spiritual self-actualization, high frequency, or high-potential state. This is a state beyond transitory happiness to fulfillment, self-worth, and integration in life. An employee or business operating on the Love To level has inspiration, consistent growth, and long term vision. In the 1:1 level, individuals are awakened and purposeful. They act with intent from inspiration within, instead of reacting from emotions without. It is no longer a mystery of how to bring the highest-charged, energy-dissipating emotional states into a balanced, unconditional love, or a 1:1 ratio. In chapter 5, I will introduce *The Quantum Collapse Process*™.

2. Choose To Level - 2:1 Ratio

Choice symbolizes the power of the educated mind to decide on a course of action based on reasoning. It involves accepting the benefits and the drawbacks leading to a more self-fulfilling life. Choice means operating more proactively than reactively. We can choose to deny the equilibrium of the universe and attempt to avoid pain and seek only pleasure, or we can choose to master the seven areas of life using pleasure and pain as fuel to complete our mission.

This level is marked by temperate emotional rhythms. For example, when costly, or even tragic, mistakes are made in any area of life, we respond not by being a victim or going off on a tirade of blame, but by creating policies and contingencies, personal or professional, in an attempt to prevent or minimize similar future occurrences.

3. Desire To Level – 3:1 Ratio

Human desire is the unquenchable thirst of the senses primarily for the pleasures of life, with an acute awareness of avoiding the associated pain. The perennial attempt to satisfy the lower-mind sense organs (the physical body) leads to the attachment of a person's self-esteem to his desires. "Nothing of the senses satisfies the soul," said Henry James.

Being in the Desire To level means being less susceptible to the extremes of life when your mission determines what your desires are. In this level, there is a high potential for strong self-worth and deserving feeling, allowing for a greater focus on mission, purpose, and goals.

4. Want To Level – 4:1 Ratio

Wants are the irrational states of illusion whereby people, places, and things are pursued without forethought of the accomplishment or achievement of a goal. This means wanting pleasure for the sake of pleasure. Wants are usually gut-level urges to bring to fruition ideals hatched through lower-mind consciousness and is based on personal or social values ("keeping up with the Joneses"). In the Want To level, people usually operate on a wish list rather than a goal list. Self-worth is attached to and dependent upon outside influences. An employee or business in the Want To level will accomplish short-term goals effectively but, will plateau. This level is marked by moderate emotional swings. An example of this is the buyer's remorse that sets in when a purchase is made for immediate gratification rather than as part of a long-term vision.

5. Need To Level – 5:1 Ratio

Called by some the "I need" disease, the perceived need of the individual overrides the reasoning mind. The ability to comprehend the actual versus the perceived is hampered by emotions. Needs are closely related to emotions, and the attainment of these needs are more a source of deep emotional security than true necessity. People in the Need To level will tend to go off on low-priority tangents, fulfilling the mission of others and ignoring their own. The "I need" disease fuels Emotional and financial bankruptcy. This level is marked by wide emotional swings. An example of this is the shock, anger, low self-worth, and blame felt by a person furloughed by a company after 25 years of *loyal service.*

6. Ought To Level - 6:1 Ratio

Life activities in the Ought To level are driven by fear, guilt, and the acceptance of others at the expense of self. The part of life spent pleasing others and in guilt-driven activities is done primarily out of the fear associated with a state of survival. The more we act in the survival mode, the more we draw people and events into our lives that create crisis. This level is marked by extreme manic and depressive emotional swings. An example of this is the person who is devastated after the get-rich-quick investment he was infatuated with goes under.

The lowest function possible for the human species is to behave in a manner intended to cause harm directly or indirectly to the self. It is referred to as a state of desperation, or the suicidal state. People stuck in the Have To level live life on the defensive. There are extreme and often violent emotional swings of elation or depression. An employee or business in the Have To work level will plateau and eventually will lose business. People living in the Have To or Got To level have the potential for self-manifesting many diseases, including cancer. This level is also the extreme state where murder and suicide take place.

The Seven Levels–Have To, Ought To, Need To, Want To, Desire To, Choose To, and Love To–reflect the level of conscious awareness you have attained. All events in all seven areas of life have the potential to be experienced in any of the levels of awareness. There is no right or wrong, only what is as it is, the perfection. The fact that you are reading this book suggests that you are seeking a more balanced, steadied, and fulfilling life experience. The evolution to higher levels of conscious awareness has a direct effect on your ability to expand your consciousness and grow to new domains of personal and professional management. In business and in life, you cannot efficiently manage and grow beyond your current responsibility level unless you rise above your emotional reactions. Your managerial competence corresponds to your ability to break through to higher levels of awareness. This occurs when you take on and manage the higher levels of emotional stress associated with greater responsibilities. At each breakthrough to a new level of awareness, there is an appreciation for the place that you have been and a greater understanding of the new challenges and responsibilities you will face. So, your life is not meant to get easier, it is meant to take on new and greater responsibilities. This is the pathway to self-fulfillment and self-worth. This is the purpose of *The Law of Sevens.*

You cannot go where you desire to go until you know where you are.

The Seven Levels

Evaluate the level of conscious awareness (1:1 Love To – 7:1 Have To) associated with the people and events in the seven areas of your life. Remember that the more emotionally charged you are about a person or event, the farther down the hierarchy of needs you are from inspiration to desperation (1:1 – 7:1).

For example, in the Mental Area, Bill charges you emotionally because he is brilliant (your perception) and you are not (your perception). To the extent that you put Bill up and put yourself down is the level of awareness that you have attained so far in this instance.

Mental Area

Person/event ___Bill___ Level of awareness _5:1 Need To_

Spiritual:

Person/event_____ Level of awareness _____

Person/event_____ Level of awareness _____

Person/event_____ Level of awareness _____

Mental:

Person/event_____ Level of awareness_____

Person/event_____ Level of awareness_____

Person/event_____ Level of awareness_____

Vocational:

Person/event_____ Level of awareness_____

Person/event_____ Level of awareness_____

Person/event_____ Level of awareness_____

Financial:

Person/event_____ Level of awareness_____

Person/event_____ Level of awareness_____

Person/event_____ Level of awareness_____

Familial:

Person/event_____ Level of awareness_____

Person/event_____ Level of awareness_____

Person/event_____ Level of awareness_____

Social:

Person/event_____ Level of awareness_____

Person/event_____ Level of awareness_____

Person/event_____ Level of awareness_____

Physical:

Person/event_____ Level of awareness_____

Person/event_____ Level of awareness_____

Person/event_____ Level of awareness_____

Action: Develop an action plan to raise your awareness one level as it relates to the people and events just listed. (For instance, if you are in the Need To level in the financial area, develop an action plan to save more and spend less until you have fewer emotional charges and more stability in the financial area.)

_____

_____

_____

_____

_____

_____

_____

_____

_____

_____

_____

_____

Loyalty, Inspiration, and Productivity

One of the best ways to raise our level of consciousness is to create alignment in our relationships. The forms that follow are designed to bring congruency and balance into the employee/employer relationship. They can be used in any form of relationship because the principles are the same.

1. On Employee/Employer form A, in the left-hand column, list a job description.

2. In the far right-hand column, list your highest values, which you determined in chapter one.

3. In the middle columns, list 10 benefits of how performing that job description serves you in obtaining your highest values.

4. Fill the page, and as many pages as it takes, until you see how your current vocation serves your life and you are inspired and appreciative toward it.

5. On form B, in the left-hand column, list your top values again.

6. In the far right-hand column, list the highest values of the employer/owner.

7. In the middle columns, list 10 benefits of how by helping your employer/owner obtain their highest values helps you obtain your highest values.

8. Fill the page and as many pages as it takes to realize that you obtain your goals only by helping others obtain their goals.

EMPLOYEE/OWNER MOTIVATION PRODUCTION LOYALTY FORM A

Job Description	Benefits	Employee Hierachy of Values
	1 6	
	2 7	
	3 8	
	4 9	
	5 10	
	1 6	
	2 7	
	3 8	
	4 9	
	5 10	
	1 6	
	2 7	
	3 8	
	4 9	
	5 10	
	1 6	
	2 7	
	3 8	
	4 9	
	5 10	
	1 6	
	2 7	
	3 8	
	4 9	
	5 10	
	1 6	
	2 7	
	3 8	
	4 9	
	5 10	

SPIRITUAL   MENTAL   VOCATIONAL   FINANCIAL   FAMILY   SOCIAL   PHYSICAL

EMPLOYEE/OWNER MOTIVATION PRODUCTION LOYALTY FORM B

Employee Hierachy of Values	Link to Company Values		Company/Owner Heirachy Values
	1	6	
	2	7	
	3	8	
	4	9	
	5	10	
	1	6	
	2	7	
	3	8	
	4	9	
	5	10	
	1	6	
	2	7	
	3	8	
	4	9	
	5	10	
	1	6	
	2	7	
	3	8	
	4	9	
	5	10	
	1	6	
	2	7	
	3	8	
	4	9	
	5	10	

SPIRITUAL   MENTAL   VOCATIONAL   FINANCIAL   FAMILY   SOCIAL   PHYSICAL

Outer motivation is a stepping stone, which can become a stumbling block, to learning the skills necessary for self-mastery and inner motivation.

Chapter 3

The Seven Skills

1. Blueprinting

2. Masterminding

3. Networking

4. Action Planning

5. Organizing

6. Re-evaluating and Recharging

7. Integrating

The Seven Skills are the special tools a master utilizes in order to create a masterpiece. I met a man in Washington State who built a 3,000-square-foot house without using a nail. It was completely tongue and groove. He was a master woodworker, and his home was an extraordinary work of art. Invest yourself in mastering the Seven Skills step by step, methodically. They are the tools of the masters of personal and professional management. Apply them to all seven areas, and they can serve you for a lifetime.

1. Blueprinting

Blueprinting, or life-planning, means putting the design and detail for your life in writing. Just as it would be unthinkable to undertake a construction project without plans, your divine design for the life that you are called to create requires a written plan. Blueprinting is more than just goal setting. It is more like mapping out with ever-finer detail the long-term plan for your life. It takes into account logistics, resources needed, stress factors affecting your design, setbacks that can occur, and contingencies. Walt Disney had plans for his life that extended 50 years into the future. You are important enough, and the world takes notice when a person has big plans. People tell me all the time, "I've got my goals in my head." "We are instant forgetters," says Mark Victor Hansen, and we can focus only on one thing at a time. Putting pen to paper does two wonderful things: it manifests from the virtual into the material; and it brings the unconscious mind into the process.

The unconscious mind is our own personal autopilot when it comes to manifesting ideas and bringing our dreams into reality. For example, if you have ever desired to purchase a new car, the car of your dreams, you will spot that car out of the corner of your eye traveling in the opposite direction on an eight-lane highway at 75 miles per hour. If you have your mind focused on a new home, you will see "for sale" signs up a side street through a clump of trees. This is the power of the unconscious mind. By blueprinting your goals and master plan, you will help unleash the most powerful instrument for manifestation on the planet, YOU!

1. Masterminding

The Master Mind principle takes effect when two or more individuals, using their creative imaginations, envision for themselves and their mastermind partners life as they would love it to be. Master Mind partners can be from any area–spouse, colleague, business partner, etc. Members meet on a weekly or biweekly basis in person or by teleconference. The members of the Master Mind join in a covenant dedicating themselves to maximum service, setting the highest example, and showing gratitude in advance for the Master Mind supplying them with the resources for a successful life. They let their minds and hearts soar without limits above the world they now know. These dreams become reality when they are captured in the form of intentions and are spoken of in the form of requests. Each member of the Master Mind commits to his partner's realization of his Master Mind requests and keeps these intentions in his heart and mind as he works to achieve his own goals. You will be amazed at the power generated by a Master Mind. The eight Master Mind principles are as follows:

1. I SURRENDER.

   I admit that, of myself, I am powerless to solve my problems, powerless to improve my life. I need help.

2. I BELIEVE.

   I come to believe that a power greater than myself–the Master Mind–can change my life.

3. I AM READY TO BE CHANGED.

   I realize that erroneous, self-defeating thinking is the cause of my problems, unhappiness, fears, and failures. I am ready to have my beliefs and attitudes changed so that my life can be transformed.

4. I DECIDE TO BE CHANGED.

   I make a decision to surrender my will and my life to the Master Mind. I ask to be changed profoundly.

5. I FORGIVE.

   I forgive myself for all my mistakes and shortcomings. I also forgive all other persons who may have harmed me.

6. I ASK.

   I make known my specific requests, asking my partner's support in knowing that the Master Mind is fulfilling my needs.

7. I GIVE THANKS.

   I give thanks that the Master Mind is responding to my needs, and I assume the same feelings I would have if my requests were fulfilled.

8. I DEDICATE MY LIFE.

   I now have a covenant in which it is agreed that the mastermind is supplying me with an abundance of all things necessary to live a successful and happy life. I dedicate myself to be of maximum service to God and to those around me; to live in a manner that sets the highest example for others to follow; and to remain responsive to God's guidance. I go forth with a spirit of enthusiasm, excitement, and expectancy. I am at peace.

3. Networking

Networking is not work if you integrate it into the seven areas. You know some people who are masters at this skill. They know everyone either directly or indirectly. They are the people you usually call when you want a recommendation for a product, service, or place to go. If you commit to your mission, the universe will send you the people and opportunities necessary to accomplish it. Most people already have a network. Occasionally, patients will tell me that they are looking for help, and within a day or two I will see someone who is looking for a new position, and I simply connect the dots. That's networking. Networking in all seven areas creates a logarithmic increase in the potential opportunities available to help you accomplish your mission. It is a way to "hedge your bet" by way of a massive universal response.

4. Action Planning

Taking action dissolves fear. Having an action plan in writing not only dissolves fear, but also promotes the confidence, self-esteem, and enthusiasm necessary to accomplish a great undertaking. Again, I cannot stress enough the brainpower brought to bear when there is a written action plan. An action plan will help keep you focused on your purpose. It assists you in creating the time for the things you love to do in life. People with action plans not only get more things done, but those things often turn out as planned. Most people spend weeks or even months planning their two-week vacation. Few people spend as much time, effort, and energy planning the other 50 weeks. Action plans work best if they are prioritized and congruent with your mission in all seven areas. If you are unsure how to write an action plan, find a mentor (chapter 4, #6) and ask, ask, ask!

5. Organizing

Being organized for some is the **only** issue in life. Lack of organization, rather than lack of skill, is at the root of most business and personal failures. You don't have to be born with fine detail orientation to be a successful organizer. The first thing is to prioritize everything you do in all seven areas. This sounds like it takes time, however, it saves time. When you take a list to the grocery store, you narrow your focus on high priorities, saving time, energy, and money. Start by cataloging your activities in all seven areas and see how that compares with your mission. For instance, if you currently spend most of your time on family, career, and finance, and your goal is to enhance your physical body, social life, and spiritual awareness, you are out of sync. This leads to self-sabotage of your growth. To avoid this you will have to re-prioritize your seven areas to increase the chances of reaching your goals. If you don't know what your mission is, simply make a list of all the things you want to be, do, or have in your life. Next, break your list down into short, medium, and long-term priorities. Your priorities will change over time. In his book, _Busting Your Rut,_ Danny Drubin says, "The key is to be the master of the change." You cannot ignore any of the seven areas of life. They are the links in the chain, the spokes of the wheel of life.

51

6. Re-evaluating and Recharging

Re-evaluating is one of the most important skills to master. The ability to measure your progress, reaffirm your course, adapt to challenges, reprioritize, and set new short-term and long-term goals equals ongoing empowerment. Every fear, doubt, and challenging situation you can or can't imagine may befall you on your journey. It helps to have an expectation reserve as large as your financial reserve. However, the time and energy invested in re-evaluating pays dividends in the form of continual momentum.

Recharging means different things to different people. I am a firm believer in taking vacations to recharge. However, if recharging for you is to rehabilitate a house or teach a class, it is great to be paid to recharge. I know someone who takes two cruises a year teaching seminars. My wife and I have a goal to take eight romantic vacations per year, as well as vacation time with family and friends. Some of these vacations can be one night at a hotel in the city, a long weekend in Europe, or just being at home for a few days with no regular work schedule. Vacations are an opportunity to read, write, and re-evaluate your mission, blueprints, goals, and action plan. Recharging can re-inspire you or change the course you've chosen.

7. Integrating

Integration is the culmination of the seven skills. It is the ability to link the seven areas of life with the mission and purpose for our life. Integration also refers to human psychology and conscious awareness. When we integrate ourselves, we rise in consciousness above our paradigms and paradoxes in order to take on new domains of self-management. When we are integrated, our mission becomes larger than our ego and the pains and pleasures of life. I like the example of a commercial jet aircraft. A commercial jet was created (its mission) to fly thousands of trips over many years and carry millions of people to their destinations. The construction and engineering (blueprinting), safety, and maintenance program (recharging and re-evaluating) are established with this purpose in mind (organizing). The individual flights are the goals in line with the mission. A jet expends an enormous amount of energy (fuel) getting off the ground. Once airborne, the energy consumption is less, and the flight plan becomes the priority (action plan). As a result of the excellent engineering and preparation of the crew, the jet can now go on autopilot (unconscious mind). On autopilot it will spend 90% of the time adjusting and re-evaluating its course, until a safe landing completes the goal. Similarly, our life's mission will encompass our entire life, and for some of us even beyond our life.

Our goals are achievable steps along the way in line with our mission. It takes a lot of time, effort, and energy to get our life off the ground. Once inspired, we have access to vast amounts of unlimited energy to maintain our course, achieve our goals, and fulfill our purpose.

The Seven Skills–blueprinting, masterminding with like inspired people, networking, creating a written action plan, organizing, re-evaluating the plan and recharging your batteries, integrating, and linking the seven areas–will align your mission with the universal laws that help lead to an inspiring and fulfilling life.

The purpose of self-mastery is self-appreciation, gratitude, and unconditional love. The result of self-mastery is fulfillment, magnetism, charisma, and outer-mastery.

Worksheet Chapter 3

The Seven Skills

Apply the Seven Skills to the Seven Areas of life.

Evaluate your current proficiency in the Seven Skills on a 1 to 10 scale (1 = not proficient; 10 = totally proficient).

Blueprinting   _____

Masterminding   _____

Networking   _____

Action Planning   _____

Organizing   _____

Re-evaluating and Recharging _____

Integrating   _____

Action:

Get coaching (Chapter 5, Secret 7) on any of the Seven Skills you rated 4 or less.

Increase your proficiency by one level or more in any of the Seven Skills you rated 5 to 9.

Begin applying the Seven Skills you rated 5 or higher to *__all__* Seven Areas of life (Integration).

Blueprinting/Life planning

Biography

You are now 90 years old. How would you have your biographer
describe your life?

_____

_____

_____

_____

_____

_____

_____

_____

_____

Your Obituary

What would a friend write about you upon your death?

Write an obituary, eulogy, or epitaph.

_____

_____

_____

_____

_____

_____

_____

_____

_____

What would you love to Be, Do, and Have?

7. List your goals in the seven areas of life.

Spiritual _____

_____

_____

_____

_____

_____

Mental _____

_____

_____

_____

_____

_____

Vocational _____

_____

_____

_____

_____

_____

Financial _____

_____

_____

_____

_____

Familial _____

_____

_____

_____

Social _____

_____

_____

_____

Physical _____

_____

_____

_____

_____

Mission Statement

1. Review your biography and obituary.

2. Review your goals in the seven areas.

3. Be thankful for what you have now and the revelations you are receiving.

4. Ask your soul what it is you are here to fulfill (your calling, mission, vision, purpose, divine design).

5. Write your mission statement in the Be, Do, and Have format.

I _____ hereby declare before myself, others, and the universe that my primary purpose is to....

Be_____

_____

_____

_____

_____

Do_____

_____

_____

_____

_____

Have_____

_____

_____

_____

_____

Affirm Your Mission

What you say to yourself has greater power than what others say to you. Your personal affirmations will program you in the direction you would love to go. Use the present tense. Use powerful and brief phrases that describe inspiring yet realistic possibilities for your life. Affirm what you smell, hear, taste, feel, and see for yourself in the future with these five senses. Link your highest goals and actions through affirmations.

"I am a genius and I apply my wisdom."

"I do what it takes to balance and integrate my family, career, and spiritual life."

"I am a master of finance and wealth building."

_____

_____

_____

_____

_____

_____

_____

_____

_____

Record your prioritized goals, mission statement, and affirmations with your most inspiring music in the background and listen to it daily!

Seven questions and seven top-priority actions

Remember that the quality of your life is determined by the quality of the questions you ask. The answers to your questions will assist you in determining your purpose and the action steps necessary to fulfill your mission.

Write and ask yourself quality questions in all Seven Areas. For example; Here are seven questions to help you uncover what you would love to do in life.

1. What is it that I would absolutely love to do?
2. How do I do what I would love to do in life and get handsomel paid to do it?
3. What are the seven highest priority actions I can do to further my objective.
4. What things could possibly get in the way and how will I handle them?
5. How do I become more efficient and effective?
6. How did no matter what happened today serve me?
7. What worked today and what didn't?

If the questions or answers don't come to you, get coaching from someone who has already accomplished what you would love to be, do, or have.

The journey of a thousand miles starts with one step.

Chapter 4

The Seven Steps

1. Mission Development

2. Gratitude and Unconditional Love

3. Balanced Perceptions (Collapse)

4. Affirmations

5. Goal Setting

6. Models and Mentors

7. Taking Effective Action

The Seven Steps are part physics, part mind science, and part wisdom. The physics and science are simple. A top automotive management consultant Paul Cummings says, "If you work them, they work every time, without fail, no exceptions!" The wisdom is in the heart and soul of the doer. That's you!

1. Mission Development

You do have a mission and you are here for a purpose. You are an integral part of this magnificent universe and you are special and bigger than you imagine. The greatest limitations on you fulfilling your purpose were, in the past, are now, in the present, and will be, in the future, imposed upon you by no one other than yourself. You are the creator of your own reality. That's the bad news. The good news is that you create limitations and therefore you can remove them.

The key to finding your mission is to open your heart and listen to the voice from within. The skills you are learning in this book can help guide you. Your individual goals and the discipline to accomplish them will be a by-product of your mission. You have a divine purpose for being on this planet in this space and time. The question for most people is what is it? Your mission, purpose, or chief aim is the foundation for all the things you do in life. Your actions in the seven areas of life will have an impact upon and can be linked to your purpose. To the extent that you are working toward your mission, you grow. When you are not working toward your mission, you decay.

Here are two great exercises to help develop your mission. One is to picture yourself at age 90 telling your life story to a biographer. Tell the story of your life, as you would love to have lived it. The other is to write your own obituary or eulogy through the eyes of a friend. The things that come up for you in these two exercises may provide you with insights into what you would love to be, do, or have in your life that you may not be working toward right now. You know your mission and purpose, although you may not have uncovered it yet. Once uncovered, your mission and purpose give rise to your goals. Your goals are not the destination. They are merely stepping-stones on the path to fulfilling your mission. Once you think you've got your mission, put it in writing in the form of a mission statement. The test of a true mission is that when you read your statement or receive your message, you experience a tear of inspiration.

2. Gratitude and Unconditional Love

Developing the skill of having gratitude for everything in the universe, as it is, puts you in tune with higher energies. In a mastermind group (page 46), members practice gratitude in advance for requests that will be fulfilled. As a child, I did not understand that both praise and reprimand were acts of love and were necessary. As an adult and a parent, I see that I am responsible for both, still receive both, and appreciate how they serve me. Gratitude enlightens and envitalizes. Ingratitude weighs us down and dissipates energy. Gratitude is maturity and brings steadiness. Ingratitude is immaturity and causes unsteadiness. Gratitude is the acknowledgement of divinity. Ingratitude is the denial of divinity. Gratitude dissolves brain noise and clears the mind for creation and inspiration.

One of the keys to discovering your mission is clearing the way for inspired ideas, the inner voice. Inspiration and purpose in the mind bring enthusiasm to the body. A person who is purposeful is on fire, and everyone around will come to watch him burn. Gratitude opens your heart to unconditional love and gives you access to unlimited resources. Unconditional love is beyond the emotion of love, which we will call *infatuation*. Unconditional love is the synthesis of dualities. When you see that the positive and negative in people and events are perfect, divine equilibrium, then you can rise above infatuation and resentment to love. The best scientific method available today for consistently achieving a state of gratitude, unconditional love, and balanced perceptions is *The Quantum Collapse Process*™.

3.   Balance Your Perceptions (Collapse)

The Quantum Collapse Process consists of a series of written questions scientifically designed to bring your emotional perceptions into equilibrium, clearing the mind for inspiration. Some of the benefits of the Quantum Collapse Process are to balance lopsided emotional perceptions, transcend stagnating states of fear and guilt, generate a greater degree of gratitude, love, certainty and presence, and turn conflict and stress into unlimited energy and vitality.

Our perceptions give rise to our emotions, and our emotions rule how we react in the pursuit of our mission. Having a balanced, even-tempered, strategic, and laser-beam focus in our approach to our mission is more effective and efficient than a positive attitude and excitement. Inspiration and enthusiasm (chapter 7) are by-products of being purposeful. Balanced perception means seeing the blessing in every crisis and the crisis in every blessing. Becoming aware of both sides of reality allows us the opportunity to integrate the events of our life into our heart and link all the areas of our life to our mission. The result of this integration is to view the world with a larger and longer-term vision, creating the calm and mental steadiness necessary to deal with the challenges you will face daily in pursuit of your mission. According to physics, the universe and life as we know it come in lightwave vibrations, or frequencies of energy. Syntropy is moving from lower-energy frequencies to higher-energy frequencies. The states of gratitude and unconditional love (by-products of the Collapse Process) are syntropic. They move us to the higher-energy frequency potentials associated with the conscious awareness necessary to create a fulfilling life.

4. Affirmations

Affirmations are spiritual and mental exercises meant to stretch and strengthen your spiritual and mental muscles - similar to physical exercise for your body. They are statements and words of power affirming to the universe that the person you would love yourself to be or desire to become is manifesting now in time and space. Dr. Larry Markson is a top management consultant and a former coach of mine. He says, "Affirmations are most effective in the present tense (I am a healthy, vital, active, and successful human being)." Affirmations are best written when you are in a state of gratitude and unconditional love and should be read each and every day at least once. Like any skill, affirmations are best learned in steps, practiced, and perfected over time. One of the benefits of having models and mentors is not having to reinvent the wheel when it comes to affirmations. Affirmations assist you in making the transition from an outer-directed person, a creature affected by emotions, peer pressure, and the opinion of others, to an inner-directed person who listens to the voice from within and is creating the life you would love to live.

5. Goal Setting

So many things have been said and written about setting and reaching goals, but just what are goals? Are they the end result? Goals are steps along the way to your purpose. Any-thing that you can achieve is a goal. Goals come alive when written and read daily. Goals should be revisited on a regular basis. All seven areas of life should be represented in your goals. Associate as many of the five senses as you can with your goals, especially sight. Use pictures, sounds, aromas, tastes, and touch to anchor your mind on reaching your goals. Goals are most effective when they are a balance of challenge and support. Goals can be anything you can envision. If you can see it, you can be it! Since goals are stepping stones, they are best written and accomplished in a graduated fashion (I am increasing sales 10% per quarter). Goals are most effective when they are written and stated in the *be, do,* and *have* rather than the *have*, *do,* and *be.* Let me explain. Many people think that when they get the things they want, they will do the things they want to do and be the person they see themselves as being. In my experience, the people who step out with certainty in their mission and purpose, gratitude in advance, presence of mind, unconditional love, and a commitment to do what-ever it takes, travel any distance, and pay any price, are the most successful. They start by being the person they see themselves as being, which attracts to them the opportunities to do the things they see themselves doing, which enables them to have the things they see themselves having.

Here are a few more ideas on effective goal setting:
Goals must be specific, clear, and detailed, not vague.
Goals must be absolute, positive, and present tense (I have, I am).
Goals must be set with realistic time frames.
Goals must be read and updated regularly.
Goals must be balanced and integrated with your values.

A person who becomes a doctor does more than become a doctor. Along the way, the person learns how to think, plan, evaluate, organize thoughts, memorize, discipline himself, and grow from the inside out.

A person who starts and develops a business must learn money management, people management, and time management. The person must become a marketer, accountant, leader, communicator, and public servant.

The most successful people (measured in all seven areas) work on themselves constantly. They consider their growth and development and that of their family priority one. Do you have a library? Do you regularly feed your mind with a vision of where you want to go? Who you want to meet? What you want to become?

A few more ideas:

♦ Find a quiet place to sit with a notepad and pencil.

♦ For 30 minutes write down every goal you have ever thought about.

♦ Spend the next hour going through your goals.

♦ Prioritize into long-term (greater than one year to achieve) and short-term goals.

♦ Circle goals for which you feel a burning desire or passion.

♦ Cross off the goals that are nice but not heartfelt.

♦ Write goals using "or more, or less, or sooner." (An example, I am earning x dollars or more by blank date or sooner. I weigh x pounds or less by blank date or sooner.)

♦ Attach reasons why you must achieve a goal. What will it mean to your family and friends and the world? What will it mean to your self-respect and self-image?

Ultimately, people will achieve more, give more, and do more for others than they will for themselves.

Post your goals up where you can read them daily.

♦ By your bedside

♦ The mirror in your bathroom

♦ Your car visor

♦ Your desk drawer

♦ The refrigerator

Keep your goals to yourself! Many people with no goals, and therefore no direction, love to make negative comments about the goals of others. Be private with your goals. Share your goals with your mastermind and other like-inspired people.

6. Models and Mentors

Models and mentors are the keys to not reinventing the wheel. They keep us on track simply by keeping a balance between being stuck in our stuff or having to do it our way and turning our life over to someone else. There is an unlimited source of models and mentors in the universe if we do not limit ourselves to space and time, past and present. Advanced training in the Quantum Collapse process makes this a possibility. Modeling means finding a successful person, past or present, and doing exactly what that person did to become successful. Reading biographies is a good source for inspiring models. Mentoring requires that you actually work with a person more in the tradition of masters and apprentices. The beautiful thing about finding a mentor is that part of being a success requires that you reach back and assist someone else in following his or her dream. Successful people are always looking for mentors and students. Once you get clear on who you are and what you would love to have, the mentor will appear. Every person is your teacher and your student. When you teach some-one or they teach you a mastered skill, you are both relearning the process.

7. Taking Effective Action

Taking effective action or, as some say, being proactive, means integrating and linking your daily activities in all seven areas – spiritual, mental, vocational, financial, familial, social, and physical –with your mission and goals. It means creating a lifestyle where there is no wasted energy, where everything you do, say, or think is in perfect harmony with your purpose, and where you are enjoying the process. When you are constantly putting out fires or spending a significant amount of your time doing things to fulfill someone else's mission, you will beat yourself up, get stressed, or make yourself ill to get you back on course. That's the divine design of the universe telling you that you are worth more than you think you are. Disease is one result of not taking effective action on your mission.

Who, What, When, Where, How, and Why?

◊   Who must you meet, know, convince, persuade, love, or befriend to move you forward in your mission?

◊   What actions must you take or not take to move you forward in your mission?

◊ When must these actions be taken or not taken?

◊ Where must you go or not go to move yourself forward in your mission?

◊ How (by what method or technique) can you proceed forward in your mission?

◊ Most important, why do you want to achieve the goals you have set?

If you have a big enough why, any goal is possible. Ask any mother or father who is working to put a child through college.

Rome wasn't built in a day, and it even took God seven days to create the universe. Neither was done without a plan. The seven steps pertain to all seven areas of life and will help guide you on the path to becoming one of a select group of people with a big enough vision to encompass them. You were not put here to be average, and you are not reading this book to be smaller. There is power and greatness within you waiting for the wakeup call that will change your world as you now know it.

Breaking things down step by step dissolves the fear and anxiety of taking on big tasks.

Worksheet Chapter 4

The Seven Steps

Evaluate your level of competence, past or present, in the Seven Steps on a scale of 1 to 10 (1 = not competent; 10 = fully competent).

Mission Development   _____

Gratitude and Unconditional Love   _____

Balanced Perceptions (Collapse)   _____

Affirmations   _____

Goal Setting and Goal Getting   _____

Models and Mentors   _____

Taking Effective Action   _____

Action:

Get coaching (Chapter 5, Secret 7) on any of the Seven Steps you rated 4 or less. Increase your competence one level or more in any of the Seven Steps you rated 5 to 9.

Begin applying the Seven Steps you rated 5 or higher to **_all_** Seven Areas of life.

The Quantum Collapse Process™

The Quantum Collapse Process assists you in bringing balance to lopsided emotions by equilibrating your perceptions concerning the people and events in your life. This is done through a series of questions you can ask and honestly answer yourself, or you may contact a trained facilitator to guide you through them.

1. Write at the top of the page the name of a person or event that is running you. This can be an infatuation or resentment, or you may perceive that you have been a victim of or have victimized someone.

2. Answer the 10 questions from form A and B completely and honestly until both pages are complete.

3. The result of this work will be a transformation of your perception of the person or event. There will be liberation from the hold this person or event had over you, as well as freedom from the fear, guilt, infatuation, or resentment associated with them.

4. Once you dissolve a highly charged, button-pushing person or event, you have the opportunity to integrate the potential energy involved. You experience the clarity of mind, certainty of purpose, and level of inspiration, enthusiasm, and vitality to the same energy level as was invested in the original charged perception.

5. The most important result is that the moment of present-time consciousness experienced propels you to the next level of conscious awareness and personal power.

6. The Collapse process is not about the people or events you collapse; it is about YOU!

The Quantum Collapse Process™ Form, Side A

Person: _____ Date: ___/___/___

Column 1 Trait I most like about them	Column 2 Initials of who see this trait in me	Column 3 How this trait in them is a drawback to me	Column 4 How this trait in me is a drawback to others	Column 5 Initials of who see the opposite trait in them

Seven Areas of Life: Spiritual Mental Vocational Financial Familial Social Physical **Think**: Past Present Future
When positives outweigh the negatives, you become emotionally attracted and infatuated (addicted).
When positives don't equal negatives, you lie. Lies are imbalances.

The Quantum Collapse Process™ Form, Side B

Person: _____ Date: ___/___/___

Column 6 Trait I most dislike about them	Column 7 Initials of who see this trait in me	Column 8 How this trait in them is a benefit to me	Column 9 How this trait in me is a benefit to others	Column 10 Initials of who see the opposite trait in them

Seven Areas of Life: Spiritual Mental Vocational Financial Familial Social Physical **Think**: Past Present Future
When negatives outweigh the positives, you become emotionally attracted and infatuated (addicted).
When negatives don't equal positives, you lie. Lies are imbalances.
When negatives equal positives, you become grateful and unconditionally loving. The truth is balance!

Ancient mysteries, science, and world religions are resources for subduing the daily distractions and expressing the inner life force.

Chapter 5

The Seven Secrets

1. Break It Down

2. Expand Your Consciousness

3. Expand Your Intellect

4. Train Your Brain to See Both Sides

5. Open Your Heart

6. Get Inspired

7. Get Coaching

As The Seven Secrets unfold, they uncover the foundation for and the details of creating yourself to be a manifestation machine. That is, these secrets, when mastered, set you apart from the herd. You become the person others seek help from as you make it clear to the world through your thought, word, and deed that you are creating the life you would love to live. You will attract into your life people, events, and opportunities that will correspond perfectly with your new level of consciousness.

1. Break it down.

Breaking everything down in all areas to its smallest components is the most effective way to start. "By the inch it's a cinch, by the yard it's hard, by the mile it's a pile", says Dr. John Demartini. Remember, it is not the destination that is of primary importance. It is the lessons you learn, people you touch, and skills you master along the way that count. Once you have mastered this skill, you will automatically and unconsciously begin to take small steps in every area based on your value system. This book is a great example. It contains seven chapters with seven parts to each chapter, an introduction, and a closing. If I had attempted to get 49 points on paper at one time, the book would not have been completed.

2. Expand your consciousness.

Expanding your mind to encompass the seven areas of life will stretch your consciousness. Once expanded, the mind cannot become small again. It is as if a light has been turned on (enlightenment), and the shadows have been revealed. Your ability to understand greater dynamics and balance stressful situations is directly related to how big a picture of the world you have. To assist you in expanding your view, it is preferable to find a mission that will go beyond your physical lifetime. Your goals in tune with this mission will necessitate a long-term vision and stretch you. Most people plan their lives based on emotions. This sets them up for failure. That is why most people depend on social security for retirement. By expanding your consciousness and rising above emotions, you set yourself up for success. The growth of consciousness has been described as going from one concentric circle to another. Once we master one level, we break through and proceed immediately to the next level of challenge. The higher we go in consciousness, the larger the circles become. The larger the circle, the greater the domains of management, magnetism, and influence. The apprentice begins his journey being consciously conscious of his **inability to** perform his craft. After a time, he becomes consciously conscious of his **ability to** perform his craft. Ultimately, the craftsman becomes unconsciously conscious of expertly performing the tasks associated with his craft. It's like driving a vehicle while eating or talking on a cellphone. Like any skill, we learn best through assimilation and accommodation, taking one step at a time.

3.　Expand your intellect.

There is a direct correlation between the books you read, the people you meet, your intellectual progress, and your fulfillment in life," says Charles Tremendous Jones. This does not mean that all intellectuals have fulfilling lives. The mental state is but one area of life. However, by immersing yourself in the writings of inspired people, you cannot escape unaffected. It has been said that insanity is doing the same things in the same way and expecting a different result. I disagree! Insanity is thinking that by continuing to do the same thing in the same way, you will continue to get the same result. Because of the principle of entropy, doing the same thing in the same way will progressively bring a lesser result over time. When you are green, you're growing; when you are ripe, you're rotting. A mind unchallenged is an invitation to deterioration. Synergy is a bringing together and building up to a higher-frequency and greater potential. It requires energy. Entropy is a breaking apart and decaying to a lower-frequency and dissipated state. It requires no energy. Which would you love to do?

4. Train your brain to see both sides.

Every action brings with it an equal and opposite reaction. One way to manage stress and balance emotions is to develop a basic understanding of the laws of physics as they pertain to emotions. Emotional highs are followed by emotional lows, or what goes up must come down. By training your brain to see both sides, you have the opportunity to live life with fewer emotional extremes. When you train your brain to see both sides, you have less of an emotional reaction and more of a rational choice about how to respond to situations. Another important factor in physics concerns energy.

When emotions are extreme, they run your life. Your focus is unsteadied, your mind is disorganized, and your energy dissipated. When your emotions are synthesized (balanced), your mind is focused, your brain is clear, and your energy is boundless.

5. Open your heart.

The more open the heart, the more of life is lived at the Love To 1:1 ratio and the Choose To 1:2 Level. The easiest route to a more open heart is through gratitude. Gratitude has been called the gateway to unconditional love. Unconditional love sits waiting in the heart. It is the light of wisdom and understanding. It is the equanimity of dualities. It is the truth and freedom that we innately seek. Imagine the difference between playing chess with time to plan strategies and think out your next move versus pinball with bells and lights blaring, with only an instant to react and no time for a plan. When you are grateful, your heart is open, your mind is steadied and organized, and you act. When you are ungrateful your heart is closed, your mind is unsteadied and disorganized, and you react.

6. Get inspired.

Inspiration is the greatest gift we can give ourselves. Physical inspiration is in the breath. When we breathe in, we not only bring the life giving gift of oxygen to our lungs, but we also set off a series of neurological stimuli that arouse the body's systems. Mentally and spiritually, we become inspired when we are doing what we love and loving what we do. If a patient tells me he or she is tired all the time, my first question is what are you inspired or not inspired about in your life right now? In most cases, we will get to some issue that is causing an emotional imbalance and blocking their ability to see the magnificence of the universe we all get to share. When we work The Quantum Collapse Process™ and they see clearly that their negative perception of an event or person has just as many positives, we start back on the road to balance and inspiration. In most cases, if you are tired, you are not inspired. The ability to inspire others or be inspired ourselves is no mystery. Simply care enough to learn the value system of the people in your life and relate to them in their value system. the more inspired you are, the more you get to do the things you love to do. The more you do the things you love to do, the more inspiration you get. By following your heart and doing what you love to do, you attract to yourself more things you love to do. Inspiration is in every cell in your body to tap into as potential energy.

7. Get coaching.

Coaching is simply finding someone who will ask more of you than you ask of yourself. The greater the level of experience and success in an area makes someone a great model, but not necessarily a great coach. The best coach is like the best teacher. It is not what is put into the student but what is drawn out of him or her. There is no limit to the coaching resources available to you. However, the universe is a big place, and you can spend your life searching. It is like surfing the internet or going to the library. You get what you would love to have when you know where to look and who to ask. There are all kinds of coaches–corporate coaches, personal coaches, relationship coaches, financial coaches, etc. Coaches serve a purpose and are worthwhile. However, until you tap into the inner coach or the inner voice, you will **need** coaching. You will attract coaches in the Need To Level 5:1 ratio. When you know your mission and follow your plan, you will attract coaches in the Desire To 3:1, Choose To 2:1, and Love To 1:1 Levels. Allow yourself to grow, and you will magnetize to yourself **inspired** coaches.

The Seven Secrets–breaking it down, expanding your consciousness and intellect, training your brain to see both sides, opening your heart, getting inspired and getting coaching–are age-old methods that prepare the soil of your mind and get you out of your own way on the journey to fulfillment and success.

The biggest secret in the universe is that there are no secrets.

The Seven Secrets

When you were a baby, no one asked you to run across the room for your first attempt at walking. They estimated your level of ability, reinforced what was comfortable to you, and challenged you to the next level.

1. **Break it down.**

In the table below, break your life down into the Seven Areas. List your top three goals in each area.

Spiritual

_____

_____

_____

Mental

_____

_____

_____

Vocational

_____

_____

_____

Financial

_____

_____

_____

Familial

_____

_____

_____

Social

_____

_____

_____

Physical

_____

_____

_____

2. Expand your consciousness.

Create positive statements in the present tense (Affirmations, Chapter 4, and part 4) that encompass your top three goals, either individually or together, in each of the Seven Areas. (For example, in the Physical Area: I am a healthy, vital, active, and physically fit person.)

Spiritual_____

_____

_____

_____

Mental_____

_____

_____

_____

Vocational_____

_____

_____

_____

Financial_____

_____

_____

_____

Familial _____

_____

_____

_____

Social _____

_____

_____

_____

Physical _____

_____

_____

_____

3. Expand your intellect.

List three methods (such as books, classes, or coaching) that will help increase your ability to accomplish your top three goals in all Seven Areas. (For example, in the Mental Area: I will read a Dale Carnegie book on remembering names and faces.)

Spiritual

_____

_____

_____

Mental

_____

_____

_____

Vocational

_____

_____

_____

Financial

_____

_____

_____

Familial

_____

_____

_____

Social

_____

_____

_____

Physical

_____

_____

_____

4a. Train your brain to see both sides.

In each of the Seven Areas, list three benefits you will receive by achieving your top goal in that area. Now list three benefits you will receive by not achieving that goal (Collapse, Chap. 4, part 3).

Spiritual Goal

_____

_____

Benefits of achieving goal   _____

                                    _____

                                    _____

Benefits of not achieving goal _____

                                    _____

                                    _____

Mental Goal

_____

_____

Benefits of achieving goal   _____

                                  _____

                                  _____

Benefits of not achieving goal _____

                                  _____

                                  _____

Vocational Goal

_____

_____

Benefits of achieving goal   _____

                                  _____

                                  _____

Benefits of not achieving goal _____

                                  _____

                                  _____

Financial Goal

_____

_____

Benefits of achieving goal   _____

_____

_____

Benefits of not achieving goal _____

_____

_____

Familial Goal

_____

_____

Benefits of achieving goal   _____

_____

_____

Benefits of not achieving goal _____

_____

_____

Social Goal

_____

_____

Benefits of achieving goal   _____

_____

_____

Benefits of not achieving goal _____

_____

_____

Physical Goal

_____

_____

Benefits of achieving goal   _____

_____

_____

Benefits of not achieving goal _____

_____

_____

4b. **Train your brain to see both sides.**

In each of the Seven Areas, list three drawbacks you will encounter as a result of achieving your top goal in that area. Now list three drawbacks you will encounter as a result of not achieving that goal (Collapse, chapter 4, part 3).

Spiritual Goal

_____

_____

Drawbacks of achieving goal   _____

_____

_____

Drawbacks of not achieving goal   _____

_____

_____

Mental Goal

_____

_____

Drawbacks of achieving goal   _____

                                 _____

                                 _____

Drawbacks of not achieving goal _____

                                 _____

                                 _____

Vocational Goal

_____

_____

Drawbacks of achieving goal   _____

                                 _____

                                 _____

Drawbacks of not achieving goal _____

                                 _____

                                 _____

Financial Goal

_____

_____

Drawbacks of achieving goal   _____

_____

_____

Drawbacks of not achieving goal   _____

_____

_____

Familial Goal

_____

_____

Drawbacks of achieving goal   _____

_____

_____

Drawbacks of not achieving goal _____

_____

_____

Social Goal

_____

_____

Drawbacks of achieving goal   _____

_____

_____

Drawbacks of not achieving goal _____

_____

_____

Physical Goal

_____

_____

Drawbacks of achieving goal   _____

_____

_____

Drawbacks of not achieving goal _____

_____

_____

Notice that accomplishing or not accomplishing goals has benefits and drawbacks. This knowledge neutralizes the infatuation with achieving goals, as well as the disappointment associated with not achieving goals. This balanced state opens the heart to inspiration, which helps create the certainty and presence of mind necessary to having your goals become stepping stones toward a fulfilling life mission.

5. **Open your heart.**

List all the people and events you are deeply grateful for in each of the seven areas until you experience a tear of inspiration.

Spiritual _____

_____

_____

_____

_____

Mental _____

_____

_____

_____

Vocational_____

_____

_____

_____

_____

Financial_____

_____

_____

_____

_____

Familial _____

_____

_____

_____

_____

Social _____

_____

_____

_____

_____

Physical _____

_____

_____

_____

_____

6. **Get inspired**.

Focus the inspired feelings of gratitude from number 5 on your top three goals in each area until your heart is open and you feel a sense of inspiration. Concentrate on the blessings, lessons, people, and events that have brought you to this place and the people you will serve as you accomplish your goals/mission. Write down any thoughts or messages that you receive while you are in this state.

_____

_____

_____

_____

_____

_____

7. Get coaching.

List the person or resource you will seek to get coaching in any of the seven areas.

Spiritual

_____

Mental

_____

Vocational

_____

Financial

_____

Familial

_____

Social

_____

Physical

_____

Fear blocks growth and evolution.

Chapter 6
The Seven Fears

1. Loss of Morals and Ethics

2. Memory Loss

3. Vocational Failure

4. Financial Bankruptcy

5. Loss of Loved Ones

6. Social Rejection

7. Disease or Death

The Seven Fears that relate to the seven areas of life are generally accompanied by the illusion that something is wrong, missing, or out of place, not as it should be, or not the way we desire. Fear has been called "False Evidence Appearing Real," by author Mark Victor Hansen. Fear has been described as an assumption in the future that you will receive more pain than pleasure from a person or event. The truth about fear is that fears both limit your progress in life and keep you safe at times. In other words, fears are not bad, and fears are not good; they serve us. Conquering fears by repressing them is one strategy for handling them. However, coming to an appreciation for the part that fear plays in your life is a more effective and lasting approach. By analyzing your fears, you will come to see how fear is harmful, helpful, and necessary. Breaking down the fears as they relate to the seven areas of life empowers you to get comfortable with an emotion that is as common in man as oxygen.

1. The Loss of Morals and Ethics

The loss of morals and ethics is said to render a person spiritually dead. Certain conditions of the mind have been called diseases of the spirit. What a person fears in relation to his moral, ethical or spiritual self depends on two sets of values. The value system of the individual determines his moral values. The collective values of the family, corporation, culture, or society determine the rules of ethics that govern the individual members. Morals and ethics change over time, and, in some cases, overnight. When one listens to his heart and lives his life inspired from within, the voices on the outside and the fear associated with conforming to societal morals and ethics become quiet. In wisdom, it is better to have the whole world against you than to have your own soul against you.

2. The Loss of Memory or Mental Illness

The loss of memory or disease and death of the mental self is perhaps a greater tragedy for some than the physical loss of life. The increase in the understanding of the body-mind-spirit connection helps bring this fear to a rational level. Many mental diseases like depression are self-induced. Depression can be described as when reality does not live up to an ideality that is false. When you have an expectation of pleasure without pain, this is a fantasy and will set you up for disappointment and depression. Due in part to the media and cultural conditioning, many people have fantasies about life. This is why antidepressants are over-prescribed and abused. Volumes have been written on mental illness, and the yearly production of psychotropic medications could fill the pyramids. This book and others like it will help pave the way for a new age in awareness and understanding of human psychology. I predict that if every human opened his or her eyes and heart and discovered their purpose for life and followed it, the incidence of mental illness would plummet.

3.   Fear of Vocational Failure

There is a fear of failure at one's chosen career or vocation. Also, there is a fear of failure in business or in performance of one's duty. The common notion that success is good and failure bad is a myth. Walt Disney went bankrupt in business several times before "Mickey Mouse Land" was founded. A large percentage of the leaders of the Fortune 500 companies have attributed their "current success" in life to difficulties, hardships, and past failures. The successes and failures of our vocational lives are here to teach us and prepare us for the next level of life. Fear can limit you or it can guide you. Fear can paralyze you or energize you. The master turns his fear into fuel to propel himself forward. Winston Churchill said, "Most of the things I feared in life never came to pass."

4. Financial Bankruptcy

This is the loss of the ability to earn a living or the loss of one's finances, home, business, car, etc. The benefit of bankruptcy is to wake us up to our true self-worth. Money is a spiritual substance measured in terms of our self-management and self-worth. Money is one method of exchange. Money is received in proportion to value given. In our society, money causes emotional extremes. People who become infatuated with or cocky about money, and people who feel like they do not deserve or have a fear of losing money, will sabotage their own efforts to grow in worth. One takes too many risks, and the other is too tight with money. These are the usual candidates for bankruptcy. You increase self-worth in relation to your ability to see both sides of the coin of life. To the extent that you desire the pleasure without the pain, for example, you will not be willing to accept the two-sided coin of life, and your self-worth will suffer. When you come to appreciate both sides of life's coin, the work and the reward, your self-worth will grow. The universe is constantly giving you opportunities in the form of lessons to build your self-worth.

5. Fear of the Loss of Loved Ones

This is the loss of loved ones through divorce, death, or abandonment, and it is another extremely emotional issue. Whole careers have been formed to help us cope with loss. Grief, bereavement, or remorse are neither good nor bad. They are a stepping stone to assist people who are stuck in the emotional abyss. The challenge occurs when the very professions created to help people actually keep people stuck in order to perpetuate themselves. As we rise up in consciousness, we begin to see how things truly are. People and events, loss and gain, are neutral until some human judges them to be otherwise. To break this paradigm, we can simply observe how the universe works and apply it to our lives. The law of thermodynamics (sometimes called the law of conservation) states that energy-matter can neither be created nor destroyed, only transformed. In the case of perceived loss via divorce, death, or abandonment, the human senses unaided are unable to see how, at the instant of perceived loss, the energy of the person missing instantaneously shows up in another form. The form can be self or other, close or distant, ~~~~~

male or female. To the extent that we emotionalize, grieve, or rejoice about what is missing is the extent to which this fear runs our lives. There is nothing missing. There is only our unwillingness to see what we perceive as missing in other forms.

6. Social Rejection

Social rejection is an overt and covert fear. Some people fear not fitting in and will go against their inner voice and submit to the outer voices. Some people fear fitting in too well or not standing out from the crowd. The outer voices are chosen from a select small group, or subculture. When people say, "I don't give a damn what others think," they are usually in an emotional state and react by going against the norm – "the rebel without a cause." Some people fear the larger backlash of societal rejection, as in a person convicted of crimes against the public trust or children. The morals and ethics of the social group you identify with will determine the peer-level of pressure, acceptance, or rejection you perceive. Some people fear that if they do what they love, they will be rejected, and that stops them. It is far better to remember that acceptance and rejection are perfectly balanced in the universe. Once you become aware that there is no greater benefit or drawback to acceptance or rejection, you will go and do what you would love to do.

7. The Fear of Physical Death or Disease

The fear of death or disease relates to a natural, accidental, or intentional loss of physical power or life force. There are many cultural mores dealing with our physical area of life. Health, appearance, weight, age, vitality, strength, and their opposites are some of them. The physical body is finite in form and is a very small percentage of our entire essence, which is infinite. We live in a very materialistic society. This explains the overemphasis on the physical and material part of life. There was another age not long ago in relative space-time when vitalism (the belief that the spiritual part of man is his true essence) was the predominant ideology. In a society where vitalism predominates, a person's spiritual assets are valued more than his or her material assets. The hierarchy of power within the culture is based on the accumulation of knowledge and spiritual energy rather than wealth. Vitalism balances materialism, and both are necessary. There is a balance of benefits and drawbacks to being attached to our physical form. The misunderstanding of the role of the body, the material world, and the essence of being human is one possible source of this fear. Remember the conservation law. There is no such thing as death. The spirit and matter that we observe as people changes form. We all "die." However, the exact amount of our spirit and matter will persist in another form sometimes recognizable and sometimes not. What we perceive as dying is simply this change in form.

We may not like it or be accepting of it, and that is also a part of our evolutionary process. Even if we are willing to accept this law to be true, we may not be willing emotionally to accept the new form. The truth is, the more we expand our vision forward , backward and outward, the more we integrate ourselves. The more we integrate ourselves, the more we understand the immortal nature of humanity. The more we understand the immortal nature of humanity, the less we fear the loss of our physical and material self.

The Seven Fears-the loss of morals and ethics, the loss of mind or memory, the fear of vocational failure, financial bankruptcy, the loss of family or loved ones, social rejection, and the fear of disease or death–are here to guide us and teach us about ourselves. We can choose to let fear run us, or we can rise above our fears and use them as fuel on our mission.

What you think about comes about. What you fear comes near.

Our illusions manifest our fears into existence. In actuality there is no fear, there are only perceptions.

The Seven Fears

What you focus on most in life is what you manifest, and what you fear comes near. Your perceptions about people and events are the root causes of any fears that control you. Understand, also, that fears have a positive side, as when your fear of heights keeps you safe from falling. To bring balance to your limiting emotions of fear, complete the following exercise.

Action:

List your greatest fear in each of the Seven Areas. Apply the principles of the Collapse (chapter 4, part 3), and train your brain to see both sides (chapter 5, part 3) by listing three benefits and three drawbacks to each fear, until you see the blessing and lesson of the fear and are grateful for having that fear.

Spiritual Fear

_____

Benefits   _____

                            _____

                            _____

Drawbacks   _____

                            _____

                            _____

Mental Fear

_____

Benefits   _____

                            _____

                            _____

Drawbacks   _____

                            _____

                            _____

Vocational Fear

_____

Benefits   _____

                  _____

                  _____

Drawbacks   _____

                  _____

                  _____

Financial Fear

_____

Benefits   _____

                  _____

                  _____

Drawbacks   _____

                  _____

                  _____

Familial Fear

_____

Benefits   _____

                   _____

                   _____

Drawbacks   _____

                   _____

                   _____

Social Fear

_____

Benefits   _____

                   _____

                   _____

Drawbacks   _____

                   _____

                   _____

Physical Fear

Benefits   _____

                         _____

                         _____

Drawbacks   _____

                         _____

                         _____

When you bring your fears into balance, they shift from limitations to inspirations (Fear to Power).

Words of power are like keywords on the Internet attracting the limitless options of the universe to you.

Chapter 7

The Seven Sacred Words

1. Wisdom

2. Gratitude

3. Presence

4. Inspiration

5. Certainty

6. Enthusiasm

7. Love

The human brain and how it acquires language is a constant source of scientific interest. Words, laughter, and music stimulate the brain, and linguistics researchers are uncovering their role in communication through the vibratory frequencies of the human nervous system. The Seven Sacred Words, or words of power, have inherent in them a vibratory frequency, almost a life of their own. Understood and practiced with intent, they represent powers that enliven the heart, mind, and soul. They are the keys to the awareness of the magnificence and magic of this world. I challenge you to imagine being consistently successful in any area of life without them.

1. Wisdom

◊ Wisdom is seeing both sides and loving what is, as it is.

◊ Wisdom is the instantaneous recognition that a crisis is a blessing. wisdom there is nothing to hold on to, nothing to change.
Life is in perfect order.

◊ Wisdom is what drops in when you have an insight that solves a
problem, adds a new dimension to your life, or reflects a new
way of being–an insight that you know is so certain you can feel
it in your gut, even though you cannot give it any rational expla-
nation. As you open your heart and mind to wisdom, you will
receive an abundant stream of new inspirations, creative thoughts
and energy.

◊ The wise man views the bigger dynamic without losing touch
with day-to-day living. He must balance a celestial consciousness with a terrestrial experience. It is easy to sit in seclusion
meditating on God, the universe, and life. Wisdom is being
purposeful when you are called to bring your inner peace,
steadiness, and certainty to a hectic world of instant gratification.

2. Gratitude

Gratitude means being grateful for what is as it is. Gratitude is a state of mind, which, once attained, opens the doorway of the heart to unconditional love. A state of gratitude allows access to the unlimited energy and power of the universe. A heart filled with gratitude has no room for resentment and cynicism. Gratitude allows us a glimpse of the blessings hidden within every perceived tragedy. When we are grateful, we are in a growth, syntropic, or higher potential state. When we are ungrateful, we are in a decaying, entropic, or lower potential state. Gratitude leads to a state of grace. When we are grateful, our mind is in an ordered, steadied, and clear condition, with the potential to be inspired. When we are ungrateful, our mind is in a disordered, unsteadied, and unclear condition, with the potential for desperation. It is our choice.

3. Presence

Presence, or present-time consciousness, is the moment when our mind is not occupied by thoughts, ideas, guilt, or blame concerning the past, or thoughts, ideas, and fears concerning the future. Being present to life is an important skill to develop. This includes paying attention to our children when they speak to us and being in the moment behind the wheel of a car. Most of life is being missed by not being in present-time consciousness. What fills our mind if not the moment of life before us? Thoughts of the future and the past make up the myriad of mental images we experience with every suggestion or question. Some say future fear and past guilt. Presence is called the love state, the balanced state, the equilibrated state, when your emotions are not running your life. When you are elated, seeing many more positives than negatives, time seemingly speeds up and flies. When you are depressed, seeing many more negatives than positives, time slows down and drags. Actually, the same amount of time passes in either situation. Emotions warp time and space. Emotions gravitate and weigh us down. Present-time consciousness is timeless and spaceless and enlightens us. Most people pursue the positive and try to avoid the negative. Both are futile and take us out of the present. When you see that every perceived negative in your life brings with it an equal and opposite positive, and every positive brings an equal and opposite negative, you enter an equilibrated, or present-time, consciousness state. In this state you see both sides of reality and appreciate your life and the events in it as part of the perfection. A master is one who has the ability to achieve this present-time consciousness state consistently. Developing our mission and setting goals while in present-time consciousness elevates us to a higher frequency vibration and energy state. This increases the potential for finding our true purpose and attracting to us the things we seek.

4. Inspiration

Physical inspiration breathes life into our lungs and body. Inspiration in the mind creates a state in which the brain is quiet, the heart is open, and the voice from within speaks louder than the voices from without. Inspiration creates action from the inside as opposed to reaction to the pressures from outside. I have great admiration for people who force themselves to overcome their fears. They act on faith, sometimes risking it all for the freedom they see at the end of the rainbow. However, this is usually done in a highly charged emotional state, which creates stress. When people are inspired, listening to the inner whisper, the emotions are balanced, they are in the present, and the fire of their purpose melts the fear away. They no longer have the stress related to overcoming fear. They have received the greatest gift known to man, the certainty of an inspired vision from the soul. The response of our body to the inspiration process is a stimulation of the nervous-system functions and an awakening of consciousness. This effect occurs if the inspiration is physical (breathing) or mental (imagination).

5. Certainty

He who has the most certainty rules! Certainty is not just confidence, bravado, or a bluffing, poker-faced I've-got-the-cookie smile.

Certainty is the knowing that you know–that you know. The deeper knowledge that comes with wisdom and experience is the source of certainty. One method of achieving certainty in our lives is by following the path set forth in this book. The balanced emotions, resolve, and focused goals of a "man on his mission" create a certainty that vitalizes us like no pseudo-emotions can. The expression, "who you are shouts so loudly, I can hardly hear what you are saying," speaks true of the person who has a certainty birthed from an inner vision and knowledge. When the heart is open, the mind is clear and present, and the message is delivered with divine certainty. True certainty is the result of balanced emotions, inner vision, organized thinking, and a plan of action.

6. Enthusiasm

Enthusiasm is the grease that helps to turn the wheels of accomplishment. Enthusiasm is what happens to the body when the mind is inspired. It is the body's motor response to, and the by-product of being inspired and on a mission. Enthusiasm is that certain something that makes us great, that pulls us out of the mediocre and commonplace, that builds power into us. It glows and shines; it lights up our faces. Enthusiasm is the keynote that makes us sing and makes men sing with us. Enthusiasm is the maker of friends, the maker of smiles, the producer of confidence. It cries to the world, "I've got what it takes." It tells all people that our job is a great job, that the company we work for just suits us, that the goods we have are the best. Enthusiasm makes us "wake up and live." It puts spring in our step, joy in our hearts, a twinkle in our eyes, and it gives us confidence in ourselves and our fellow humans.

Enthusiasm changes a deadpan salesman into a producer, a pessimist to an optimist, a loafer to a go-getter. If we have enthusiasm, we should thank God for it. If we don't have it, then we should get down on our knees and pray for it.

7. Unconditional Love

I do not define love as an emotion. It deserves a greater place in human reality. Love is the transcendence of emotion. It is the highest-frequency spiritual state possible for human consciousness. Love is the equilibration of the duality of human emotions. Love is the answer to all questions.

Omnia Vincit Amour - Love conquers all. (Virgil)

The entire universe is an expression of love in the form of light. In theology, one definition of the word divinity is "an emanation of light." Science defines this high-energy state as the full-quantum state.

The universe is 99.9% lightwave particles (photons). The elements hydrogen, helium, calcium, etc., of the periodic table that make up our bodies and all the other matter in our world and beyond are, in effect, less than 1% of the universe. These elements are understood now by scientists to be light frozen in atomic-mass densities.

When matter–positively or negatively charged ions–is brought into the neutral state, it transforms into light. Matter becomes light, which is spaceless, timeless, massless, chargeless, and present-time consciousness. When light energy is dissipated into a positive and negative-charged ionic state, it becomes matter, which has space, time, charge, and mass, and past and future consciousness. Therefore, matter has the potential to merge positive and negative-charge ions to become light, and light has the potential to dissipate into positive and negative-charge ions or matter. Light energy to matter, matter to light energy. Love is the transforming force from matter to energy.

The human sensory system will perceive people and events as one-sided, either positive or negative (judgment). The master is one who sees the positive and negative in every person and event and rises above this paradox to the next level of conscious awareness. The ability to see both sides and appreciate with humbleness and awe the magnificence of the universe we live in, lifts us to a place beyond opinion and clears the mind for inspiration and the resultant enthusiasm of the body. You have the potential to unleash the power of the universe in your life with the comprehension of this love principle.

Love is appreciating both sides of every event as a gift from God. It is loving the person who is putting the gold in your hands or nails in your coffin. A desire to love and be loved is as natural to the human species as being responsive to light. Giving and receiving love are as natural as breathing in and out. We breathe in the light and love energy from the source and breathe out the light and love energy to others. You cannot give love without receiving love, nor can you receive love without giving love. Love is order, balance, and present time. When we bring order to chaos and balance our emotions, we become present and we have access to the unlimited light and love energy of the universe. When we bring chaos to order and imbalance our emotions, we move into fear and guilt, we weigh ourselves down, and we dissipate and limit our energy. Gratitude is the gateway to open the heart to love and light. Ingratitude is the pathway to gravitation and closes the love light within the heart.

The Seven Sacred Words–wisdom, gratitude, presence, inspiration, certainty, enthusiasm, and unconditional love–are words of power and gifts we receive to remind us of who we are, where we came from, why we are here, and where we are going. We are terrestrial and celestial, we are body and soul, we are matter and spirit. We are stars, we came from stars, we are here to love unconditionally, and we will return to stars.

Modern linguistics scholars have discovered that what we say to others is a reflection of our own inner conversation.

The Seven Sacred Words

Wisdom, Gratitude, Presence, Inspiration, Certainty, and Enthusiasm (parts 1-6) are by-products of Unconditional Love (part 7). Unconditional Love is having balanced emotions and a balanced, loving thinking regarding the people and events in your life.

Action:

1. Write down the name of the person or event that you have the most emotional charges toward in each of the Seven Areas of life.

2. Balance these charges by listing three benefits and drawbacks following the steps to the Balanced Perceptions of the Collapse Process (chapter 4, part 3) and the Secret to Train Your Brain to See Both Sides (chapter 5, part 4).

3. When the emotional charges are completely balanced, you understand that the people you despise or think have harmed you are your teachers, and the events you perceived as negative were blessings given to you. You will be thankful for having that person or event in your life, and you will be in an inspired state in present time. Your mind will quiet, and you will receive a message of pure wisdom regarding your

future action toward this person or event. (Write it down.)
You will have certainty in this course of action, and your
body will respond with the enthusiasm of a person on a
purposeful mission.

Spiritual

Person or

Event_____

Benefits   _____

_____

_____

Drawbacks   _____

_____

_____

Message

_____

_____

_____

_____

_____

_____

_____

Mental

Person or Event _____

Benefits   _____

    _____

    _____

Drawbacks   _____

    _____

    _____

Message

_____

_____

_____

_____

_____

_____

_____

Vocational

Person or Event _____

Benefits   _____

_____

_____

Drawbacks   _____

_____

_____

Message

_____

_____

_____

_____

_____

_____

_____

Financial

Person or Event _____

Benefits _____

_____

_____

Drawbacks _____

_____

_____

Message

_____

_____

_____

_____

_____

_____

_____

Familial

Person or Event _____

Benefits   _____

_____

_____

Drawbacks   _____

_____

_____

Message

_____

_____

_____

_____

_____

_____

_____

Social

Person or Event _____

Benefits   _____

                _____

                _____

Drawbacks   _____

                _____

                _____

Message

_____

_____

_____

_____

_____

_____

_____

Physical

Person or Event _____

Benefits _____

_____

_____

Drawbacks _____

_____

_____

Message

_____

_____

_____

_____

_____

_____

_____

Repeat this process for the next most highly charged person or
event in all Seven Areas, until you have balanced or neutralized all
of your emotional charges. At the end of this process, you will have
a new perspective on the issues in your life, as well as a definite
course of action you can take to help fulfill your dreams.

Congratulations! You have just completed a comprehensive course of study in personal development and universal principles. The information referenced here is voluminous, both literally and experientially. The greatest potential for growth and learning occurs when there is a balance of assimilation and accommodation. Some of the material here was practical and easy to comprehend so that you could assimilate it. Some of the material here was theoretical and hard to comprehend so that you could accommodate to it. The next step is to review and reread *The Law of Sevens* and start working.

Addendum I

The Seven Questions

The quality of your life depends on the quality of the questions you ask yourself.

1. How do I do what I love to do and have a fulfilling spiritual life?

2. How do I do what I love to do and have a fulfilling mental life?

3. How do I do what I love to do and get handsomely paid?

4. How do I do what I love to do and create financial abundance?

5. How do I do what I love to do and have a fulfilling family life?

6. How do I do what I love to do and have a fulfilling social life?

7. How do I do what I love to do and keep my physical health?

Your brain will respond to every question it is asked. You can ask self-defeating questions, such as, "Why am I so stupid?" or "Why can't I get ahead?" Or you can craft your own questions like the seven questions above. I know that by now you will choose the seven questions.

Addendum II

The Seven Facets of Health Potential and Weight Management

What is health?

Webster's Dictionary defines health as a condition of wholeness in which all of the organs are functioning 100% all of the time. Symptoms or the lack of symptoms is not a true barometer of one's state of health or sickness. Also, degree or intensity of pain is not a measure of health. A splinter or toothache may cause severe pain, and a serious disease may only cause slight discomfort.

Dorland's Medical Dictionary defines health as a state of optimum mental, physical, and social well being and not merely the absence of disease or infirmities. Judging our state of health by our symptoms or lack of symptoms is a dangerous game. The practice of masking symptoms with pills, potions, or lotions is an extension of this dangerous way of thinking.

Health can be described as being synonymous with function. How do we determine if we are healthy? Optimizing the seven facets may enhance health potential:

1. Genetics
2. Nutrition
3. Exercise
4. Attitude
5. Rest
6. Biomechanics
7. Nerve Supply

144

1. Genetics

We cannot choose our parents and save for the coming of genetic engineering we each start life with a genetic predisposition.

One seventh of our health potential is determined by genetics

2. Nutrition

"You are what you eat" is an old adage that is true. The food that you eat is the fuel your body uses to reproduce cells. Nutrition can be described as the food you eat, the air you breathe, the water you drink. The basics of nutrition are simple. The earth is over 70% water. The human body is over 70% water. Water is the universal solvent. The majority of the foods we eat should be water foods. Water foods are fruits and vegetables. The intake of dairy & meat products should be minimized. Breads should be the whole grain variety. Never put yourself on a diet because diets don't work! The first three letters in diet are d-i-e and we don't want that. Cheating is allowed. If you want that delicious desert - order it - have a spoonful - satisfy the craving and push the rest away. Overindulge in moderation. Supplementation is a two way street. Over use, improper, or poorly produced supplements can be a poison to your body.

One seventh of our health potential is determined by nutrition

3. Exercise

It is essential to move all body parts in their proper range of motion on a regular basis. Exercise is essential as a balancing tool. If your lifestyle or occupational demands cause you to perform repetitive motions then exercise in the opposite ranges of motion will bring about the balance necessary to sustain a healthy body over many, many years. There are two types of exercise: passive & active. Passive exercises: walking, swimming, Tai Chi, Yoga. Active exercises: running, weight-lifting, contact or competitive sports. We each require a little bit of both to balance our bodies. In sports it is essential to do sport specific exercises in order to optimize performance and minimize injury.

One seventh of our health potential is determined by exercise

4. Attitude

In nutrition, you are what you eat. In attitude, you are what you think. The most significant mental aspect of health potential and weight management in an affluent society is attitude and emotional balance. Lopsided emotional charges, infatuation and resentment, fear and guilt, distorted memories and imagination, and the blame and victim game are at the root of disease, especially obesity. They affect hormonal balance, disrupt metabolism, weigh us down, and become the baggage we carry in our minds and bodies. Many individuals have no destination or plan and many others have abandoned their plan for the desires of the senses. They are sheep being led to the final slaughterhouse. The fact that you

146

are reading this book says that you are on a mission, listening to a calling, or inspired to find a way to do what you love and love what you do. The Quantum Collapse Process in Chapter 4 is a methodology for neutralizing lopsided emotions and bringing a balanced loving state to the mind and body. This allows the inner voice to rule and not the outer voices, freeing the mind to focus on your mission and the body to function at a higher metabolic and hormonal efficiency. Attitude is the **_result_** of man's innermost mental and spiritual state. Vitality is the **_result_** of inspiration of mind. If you are chronically tired you are not inspired. If you are chronically overweight you are off purpose.

One seventh of our health potential is determined by attitude

5. Rest

Rest is essential to replenish the body's resources. When we sleep the heart and lungs slow down. All of the organ systems of the body slow down. This allows the brain to devote more energy to the replenishing and healing process. Improper rest causes mental, emotional, physical and chemical fatigue which down-grades the quality of life and decreases the ability of the nervous system and the Immune System to protect the body from injury & disease.

One seventh of our health potential is determined by rest

6. Biomechanics

Biomechanics involves the structure of our body and the way in which we use it. Most importantly we must focus on posture. Posture is the foundation and starting point for the body's ability to adapt to external invasive forces. Special attention must be given to our posture and the proper mechanics of body movement in normal activities of daily living. Think of your body as a tool. If you use it improperly or use it in activities for which it was not designed you risk damage, decreased function, and possibly death.

One seventh of our health potential is determined by biomechanics.

7. Nerve Supply

The nervous system controls all the functions of the body - it is responsible for transmitting the life force. It is made up of the brain, spinal cord & nerve bundles, which communicate with all the cells. Interference to the nerve supply is the primary cause of imbalance in the body. Physical, chemical, and emotional stressors are the primary cause of interference. Restoration of the nerve supply is necessary for true healing to occur. The goal of chiropractic, massage, acupuncture, naturopathy, and all holistic health fields is to return the body to balance. Returning the balance using natural methods is most effective.

One seventh of our health potential is determined by nerve supply

The seven facets we have just mentioned are like the spokes of a wheel - all must be functioning properly. Reaching our peak health potential and managing weight is a journey. It requires three things: desire, information, and common sense. Most people are desirous of living a balanced and healthy life. The information provided above is adequate. Overindulging in moderation as it applies to each of the facets of health is a common sense approach.

Addendum III

The Seven Circles of Selling

It has been said that nothing gets done in the world until a sale is made. Selling or being sold is often considered a negative when in fact the equal exchange of goods and services is a key to fulfilling the dreams of both buyer and seller. We will at some level and in some form spend our entire lives selling our products, services, and ideas. To exchange something of value to others for something of value to you is a circular and spiritual event.

1. Know with certainty and have FCB (faith, confidence, and belief) in your PSI (products, services, and ideas) and market.
2. Introduce yourself, your product, and establish rapport.
3. To sell is to ask, so ask questions to identify voids and values.
4. Clarify and confirm the void, offer a solution and congruent value.
5. Overcome objections and close with a commitment.
6. Fulfill your commitment beyond expectations.
7. Be thankful to and for your PSI, the clients they allow you to service, and ask for referrals.

Completing the circle of the sale (win, win) not only accomplishes a task, it enriches both buyer and seller, re-enforces the spiritual law of fair exchange, and provides the inspiration for a rise in human potentiality and consciousness.

Addendum IV

The Seven Signs of the Sheep

In a low-tech society there is a tendency to control and keep the masses in ignorance through fear and tyranny in order to keep control. The manipulation of the masses through the media and the marketplace is also one of the drawbacks of a high tech society. The problem is when there is mass ignorance, (everyone has been fed the same predigested information) how do we know we are being treated like sheep?

The seven signs are:

1. You buy your café-latte at Starbucks.
2. You believe drug makers are in business to make people healthy.
3. You brag about standing in line for three hours at Disney.
4. You believe you will lose weight by eating "fat free" products.
5. You believe that the purpose of marriage is to make people happy.
6. You believe that money is either the route of all evil or the key to a happy life.
7. You think the models on exercise infomercials actually got so fit and sculpted by using the apparatus they are selling.

The seven signs of the sheep are not a criticism; they are a wakeup call to the myths and lies we love to buy and the reality that we face. It is easier to stay asleep, however, more fulfilling to wake up to the dance of life.

151

Acknowledgements

The Quantum Collapse Process™ is a copyrighted and trademarked scientific methodology created by Dr. John Demartini.
For information, call 888-DEMARTINI or log on to

.

Goal-setting ideas and tips were taken with permission from articles written by Dr. Lawrence Neuman, Esq.
For more information, call 215-805-1003.

Mastermind principles reprinted with permission from The Master Mind Journal, produced and distributed by the Church of Today.
For information, call 800- 256-1984, .

Affirmations, Dr. Larry Markson, Chiropractic Practice Management In Action, The Masters, 2001 Marcus Avenue, Suite W95,
Lake Success, NY 11042
For information, call 800-451-4514.

Fear, Mark Victor Hanson and Associates, Inc., P.O. Box 7665,
Newport Beach, CA 92658-7665
For information, call 800-433-2314.

Mastering Change, Dr. Danny Drubin, 4th Dimension Management
Corporation, P.O. Box 27740, Las Vegas, NV 89126
For information, call 877-540-4600,   .

Paul D. Cummings, Worldwide Enterprises, Motivational speaker
and Trainer, 1860 Pope Creek Road, Wildwood, GA 30757

Charles "Tremendous" Jones, 206 West Allen Street,
Mechanicsburg, PA 17055, For information, call 800-233-2665,
www.executiveBooks.com

If you desire more information about _The Law of Sevens_, _"The Law of Sevens Training Program"_ or any other programs, inspirational books and CD's.

Contact Dr. Daniel Lavanga at:

Wizdom At Work
112 East Pennsylvania Boulevard
Feasterville, PA 19053
Phone: 215-364-1112
Fax: 215-364-3231
E-mail: drlavanga@aol.com